T0273190

Structure of the Embryonic Rat Brain

Structure of the Embryonic Rat Brain

christopher janke

FENCE BOOKS

The following poems in this book originally appeared in:
Structure of the Embryonic Rat Brain   *Spinning Jenny*
Structure of the Embryonic Rat Brain 2   *Fence*
Structure of the Embryonic Rat Brain 3   *blazevox*
Structure of the Embryonic Rat Brain 5   *blazevox*
Structure of the Embryonic Rat Brain 9   *Fence*
Structure of the Embryonic Rat Brain 10 *Goodfoot*

This book is dedicated to my father.

With great thanks to my mom, sister, and to Emily.

And thanks to the many poets who helped me with the poems in this book and to the po-group for letting me know when I'm full of it.

Published in the United States by
Fence Books
303 East Eighth Street, #B1
New York, NY 10009
www.fencebooks.com

Fence Books are distributed by
University Press of New England
www.upne.com

Fence Books are printed in Canada by
Western Printing Group
www.westcanpg.com

Author photo by Emily A. Brewster
Front cover design by Winans Creative
Front cover photo by Peter Nguyen
Book design by Amy Borezo, shelter/Books
Drawings by Catherine Janke

Library of Congress Cataloging in Publication Data
          Janke, Christopher
          Structure of the Embryonic Rat Brain / Christopher Janke

Library of Congress Control Number: 2007922312

ISBN-13: 978-1-934200-00-1
ISBN-10: 1-934200-00-X

FIRST EDITION

"I'm a rat. See my tail?"

– Jim Jones (from New Medico at Lennox Hill)

What kind of knife? What kind of throat? What steel? Who cuts the warp?
Who scissors through? Who pins the paws? What kind of pins? What color?
What creature? Who slices a head? What gory miracle? What unanimated
gelatinous—dead-pink & fatty. What kind slices? What kind
peers? What kind slices?

Plumbers, street-sweepers, what kind of sewing machine operators, of xerox
repair women carefully adjusting their undergarments, what kind of astronauts,
of small-framed sex-shop proprietors, what kind of baseball pitchers, of welders
and shoddy artists and greasy mayors.

The mind, my horse, I, its awkward saddle, leather-riven and awl-holed, my seat
a shining star of sludge, dirt and oil, muck, how I move my arms, how I reign

the weather, how I am a tree, how I shine and shine, what kind of light escapes, glossy, small light of dark light.

On the left. Marionette strings drawn up into a star-joint called brain. A rope to each hair on the head, to each end of each earth, floss running down my spine, yourself tied to the back of yourself, tied to the pickle of the world, the universe hunched over and begging to carry you, your heavy-eye-stones.

Why not map with ragged teeth? Why not gray barely-matter for the loose-fitting unholdable fabric, for the gown made of water? Doors flung open on a rat. Tied to the table with the universe inside. Spread-eagle mind. No million-year hurling itself. Inside, how the rat once beheld me, fractured, refracted me. We brothers. We pins to hold down space.

What kind of creature says mind. Says marrow, says bone, says theory of squish, lands his pieces in a decorative fashion, bets on the 8, fans his tail to attract her, or her, what kind chats about napkins and loses a divinity in the drawer, what kind throws sneakers over a wire, sits at a telescope and demands a hammer.

In the morning, formaldehyde, the amniotic fluid for the body out of the world. The doctor combs the muted rat with her fingers. What electric non-compliance, what string-streaked cheeks, what glimmer of preservation, what laws of matter, doctor, what faith, what horror of steel, what glory of the kingdom, what king of rodents, what crown, what broken, what opened, what mind to peer at mind, what god gives breath to the god that gives breath.

What welder in a field of poppies, what fingers in the Pacific, what fear of logic, what invidious dismantlement, what execution of the unknown, what rubs itself cat-like, where are the puddles, where is the aardvark with the yellow eyes who hid and watched his prey until its delicacy brought it to tears.

What rat dream. What blind children. What pink nubs like scars come to life.

What world of lessening what slow cultivation what exercise of muscle of cement what blind desire in a mine field at dusk with a few stars and a vague sense of the beloved on the other side waving her arms what a disciplined tree what a jubilant rhododendron what fallacy what discretion what error what self-control what rat in a maze inside a rat

what great space hurling through great space what ingenious dead planet what urge like following a string what taste like chalk what shoulders what arms what strength what height what sky what star what fear what fall what which-way-up what what-way-down what broken what desperation what rat

Which new world, what delight in discovery, what white-like-sand-but-lighter-and-you-can-eat-it, what holy. What acetaminophen, what glossary, what making peace, what long-handled me, doctor, this rat has dread in its heart—doctor, the pins—doctor, my feet—doctor, the light—doctor, the grassy field—doctor, the rats in the stars—doctor, the stars in the rat, they thank you & thank you.

Frolicking and unattainable, a high mountain turn where the trees get shorter, where the rocks are whiter, where the goats turn and run. A long spike and repetitive piercings. A hypothetical benefit, an acute dissembling, a lawnmower floating on a lake: perdurable, prodigious, banal. O people of the desert, of the flood, of desperation and groping with intangible hands.

Unsustainable. The ribcage is sharp. I hold a paper dish. A headless and waterlogged match. I am lost at sea in a crow's nest, mad and aloft, in the beyond of beyond, on top of the fridge where I cannot reach me, to break in and not to find, for the wishing that fulfills wishing, for the General looking at pins on a map, for the endless repetition of something very narrow and impossible to hold.

Out of where the octopus strikes. And drawn to the appalling, to the full bath of the teeming grotesque, to the package of gods in kitchens—knives, yes, knives, but not only knives—to a hoof stuck between rocks, to no attribution, no charge, just a crescendo that comes not from the horns and not from the strings and a sforzando that creeps up like arms from behind.

To the earnest broom and its sweeping. To the clearing of bodies. To the web that comes before the spider. To the new breed of corn. To salmon and automatic transmission. To the dropping of life into life, for the passing on of a name for a sake that is not clear, as if every word is a buoy, as if the necessity that is not necessity is nonetheless your ever-loving sustenance.

For when you're in the herd, in the Route 9 traffic, when you're thrusting your
shoulder through a door, when I am your satellite, when you are the center with
the radio low, glaring at a sheet of numbers, when the trees themselves don
chainsaws to give you shelter, and when they don't, and when you are alone in
woods and rain wondering how you will find your glasses, or when you are on your
earthbed thinking of rats, and when the rats are thinking of you, and when the
wind lifts a whale into the air and when the whale sails around the earth and when
it speaks, and when it is as silent as a missing person, when the silence nuzzles
your side like a hungry youngling, when it seems unbound, and when you cannot
think of beyond without a sleight-of-hand, when the capricious soul lies down
with no reluctance, when what you most want is momentarily clear but vanishes

when you lift your head to look at it and see only the wall, and when you cling to that exact terror, for at the bottom is a guitar in a ludicrous howl, and when the frozen are defrosted and do not know whose kingdom they now worship and kowtow to in praise and muffled praise.

So stare and consider and stare and consider, for the water is uniform and there is no wind, and the boat is so small that even it can no longer be spoken of, for to speak or to giggle or to raise arms up high or to burst is all uniqueness or more of the same—and in the state in which the opposites are yanking on your veins outstretched, your space out of space, and here you are, halved into half of the world.

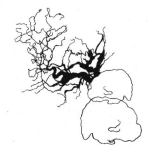

To the harmonics of alleys and the ringing in the ears and the particular cage of the self made of glass and woven wire and buttressed by sinews against the fish in the teeth and the arms and the ropes and doom and the warm fire at the crack of doom where a man paces a submarine on an ocean floor with an anxiety that is his precious vertigo though he has nowhere any further to fall but toward the sensation of the lacuna deep within.

To walk into rooms and stare at a corner one hundred times, to vagrancy, to soul—unfixed by clamp or hanger or rabbets or tied with silk sheets at the inside of the knees. To extrusions of the extranatural—debt, sport, and fleur-de-lys, to paisley and to the grand and golden amoeba embossed and put atop a castle, to rock, stick, and gizzard, to the crowbar pinging against the side, swaying like a man hung by the neck from a scaffolding by another man, one who scrutinized and squinted and gazed lovingly at every persuasion of rope, poured himself over rope with his deepest eye, his whole self thrown into hemp and cotton and silk, into waxen, polyester, and tar-filled.

What infinitely wise and eyeless man too fat to fit down the soup aisle. What architect of a coup who must now buy gloves. What congress of poets mistakenly clogging the subways with tuna fish. What deer pushing her snout into yellow leaves.

The gimbals dislodged, a spyglass and a knife, the giddyap and the dancing of the furiant, the prayer of an evil man in the year of jubilee while he forgives a debt and causes the blindness of an entire tribe, what of his hunch, his instrument board, his indestructible sense of the many knots with the name 'cat' in them, what of my unhooked ligature, my too-tight jackboot, is this the knife wielded in the boardroom, the cut of habitual introspection, is this a woman concluding in de facto that something must be done and is she striking the mailman with a switch or spraying poison on the mealy worms or just digging within herself and beginning to divide because she knows only that she must decide and she does so—speciously or entirely truly in line with a sense of the common, for she must push me ahead for I have opened a fish to distinguish between heart and liver and head, I have abused process or presence, abused substance or self, and what do I have when I am plain or jejuned and inadvertently nixed or gloriously chosen and nipped.

For the phrenologist on the top of the world scouring the surface for pure water for his throat, for a way to carve, a way to go, shall you write a constitution or take delight in a banker or carry one above your head, is your stunting from your own hand, should you build the Hoover Dam, become strong and phlegmatic, make a bolo out of your own choosing or craft a teleological talisman to hang around your neck. The crux of a mammal, the ankle of a moment, the echo of a ping and its harmonies imagined by wolves and prisoners in black skull caps, and the sound of men burying children on a hill.

The bomber confused, is this the right house, the right town, the right lover, the right body, the right head, are you the right person, do I weep over you or you over me or we over this miracle obsequious this common cliché over the heartbreak apparent and imminent and glowing quotidian, the shining of a buckle of a belt in the middle of a street under an unremarkable evening with motors humming and fingers twitching on devices and three dogs nearby out of one another's sights and can we see them slowly sniffing at the air for an aromatic path for a sign one sign any sign at all.

For Kant and harpoons and girls cutting off the tips of their toes, just the tips, for morsel and how the body. For steel and popcorn. For steam. For the wondering: what is wrong—why can't I eat—am I transformed into nothing by division—here is the mirror and here the christ and here the ever-shall-I-know-I-am-not-whole: a small toy dumptruck.

What vines through a skull, leafy, what salute to a red ocean, what implausible man, what inexhaustible wealth that is his nose, is his stone-circle path, is the descent into an infinite and incomprehensible substance or is a rising up into Japanese pigs who look to me and say boo-boo.

What vision of insouciance, what distraught pickerel, what peeling apart of a leaf unto its barest bones, what hooks of the fingers bent backwards and forwards and backwards and forwards and never breaking off, what image of a long dark road, what capitalization of I, what human drill-bit boring into an enormous blackness spraying solid black amorphous twists onto the newly paved driveway, what sign on the path that says 'path,' that says 'tree,' that says 'rock,' that says 'porcupine quills in deep melancholy,' that says 'large woman drinking cheap beer and sketching wounded gazelles,' that says 'white pavement without any cracks,' that says 'o do help me,' but there is no body and there is no body only fingerprints and a brush crusted and dried with paint.

For the trapezer. For his individual parade. For his wondering if things will only get worse. Or if perhaps his foresight is correct, that they will block off main street to praise his impossible tooth, his impossible pinky, his impossible to breathe at this height, at any height, his impossible to place on the bare back of a wasp or on the back of the jesus of a wasps' nest of jesuses, all swarming about and begging for clarity, and the queen, alone in the rain, pleading to be rid of the vision of the Great Dane staring into the eyes.

The garment too small to be worn.

The cavalier carbon-dated clams. The kissing off of the gooey makeup. The hand from the eye. The giant fly burrowing out of the earth. To place a whole city on my tongue. To rise up on ice-blades, to be brought up the spine on a system of pulleys, to have the need at the neck in a state of splendid suspension on binder's twine, to have my first touch of soil.

For the ripping and disspinning and climbing, overpowering and vehement, morning-glory-bluish against the sharp spines of the balcony, oh don't stand up there, it isn't safe, don't look down—you marvel of all time, you wonder and ill-spent, you hurling moment of blackness with awe and contemplation, with glory of sun and of knife—you starry, you mind, you heart, you miracle, you knack to undo, you dreadful, you grand and august—you you, your-self you, you heavenly, resplendent leap.

In the beginning was the rat and the rat was with god and the rat was god and the rat layed itself down to be picked at by onions. For the end or there is no end, or for the man with no description for he is not a bear and is not lipstick and is not the regularity of nature nor the fundamental pillar of all creation swinging from the stars or shaped like a curlicue.

Deeply prejudiced but gentle rat. Legislative rat. Rat beginning and ending with a bang. The lord rat running from our eating of him as he hurls all things towards their inestimable nothings, towards miracle somethings, into miracle peristalsis, miracle throat, towards Sam Dordoni in the belly of a rat. Glory be to the gravitron, to the rubber-slinged and soulful. Glory to the beard. We've come here to contemplate one life, with the Lord our rat sitting in his own stomach and chasing his tail, in a hall of mirrors in tactile 3D where you can fall into the mouth of a reflection and find deep inside another one to fall into. At the bottom of the mouth is another mouth.

For the word that changes one life.

For slim chance. For our slim chance. For the clothes in my closet to which I would set fire if I dared, to what you know that you will never tell another, for your shoes, the ones you are wearing or the ones you will wear tomorrow, and for seeing them in your mind as if they were an inch in front of your eyes, their eye-holes and blotch-stained laces, for what are the eyes that come out of nothing, like waking in a room at dusk and not knowing anything that has ever come before.

For asking not how did I get here but for saying dear creation of nothing dear in and of itself dear miracle beyond that which I can withstand, dear rat am I a fake, a faux foe, I have thrust my arm into my chest and found there is nothing to touch, nothing to feel, no jawbone and no blue man humming. For essential to the very nature of all things are some 13 impalers and their slicked-back appearance. Is this mundus sensibilis the beginning of the causality, the substratum of the thinking self, the destruction of possibility, for there is a number that begins with a one and has 32 zeros and it is the temperature above which there can be no rat, and yet for me to be saying this here and now, there must have been a rat the size of a babytooth compressed into infinite fahrenheit degrees. For I am crouched in my closet and I have lit a candle and I am speaking to my limbs which have cast a shadow over the prairie like a mountain that wants only flatness and I am saying, right now, I'm saying: we're all here. Now what do we do.

Out of nothing, a brain on pavement.

Out of nothing, pavement. Out of nothing, a silver planet, possums. Out of nothing, a road, a stream, a man stepping out into traffic, an assortment of metaphysics and a television set lying in a brook. Out of nothing, an eyesocket, a cupholder but no cup, and my optic nerve dropped down from the stars.

Flippers and flight control and inner systematic principles of pure understanding. Who presses her face against the glass and the glass is cold and she cannot tell if outside there is really a kind of absolute blackness or if there is a blackness moving by the window or a blackness so-far-out-there-that-it-is-hardly-worth-mentioning or maybe it's an old woman in a sweater twirling in moonlight in the middle of the road.

Out of nothing, the lustre of a particular hour. A blue-gray sky and indecisive snow-squalls. A quiet weatherly anticipation.

Out of nothing, a garbage man tossing a gleaming white bag into his truck. He arcs it through the air. Out of nothing, the body, he thinks, sitting up at night, when will it be swallowed, and how will I feel once the holy snakes of smoke have poured out from my every corner.

Standing high on a board, a boy is poised with his toes curled over the edge thinking of the greatest thing to which has ever been given a body and thinking of the time he stared into his dog's clouded eyes as the vet layed out his options and thinking—how does a body hold what it holds—and thinking: Now Appearing In The Center Ring As An Exercise In Imagining A Prelude To This Very Moment

In Which Women And Men Are Hanging Wallpaper And Making Curry And Are
Naming Their Sons Jim And Looking Up At The Night Sky And Saying There Is
Nothing, Do You Hear, There Is Nothing For Me, We Now Welcome: nothing, the
exercise of the infinite something that confronts like an uprooted tree floating
down a river, no world attached, inarticulate and floppy, something that hurls me
back into a basement to a time when we were crafting televisions or typefaces or
watches that need no winding or we were talking and for once we were pleased—
happy to not have what we wanted for we had a lunging towards the center or
towards the outskirts or no lunging at all for in that damp place without touching
the ball of a foot or grazing the nape of a neck, we wrangled with something in
our mouths that far from naming and in spite of all appearances made us see the
city as something other than a backdrop with a slit in it behind which everyone
is slowly slipping leaving no chance for further commerce or caress, leaving only

a parking lot filled with leaves and a sign advertising ice cream where once we licked a cone or touched a tongue to another tongue, for instead of only a favonian wind, there was something like a well dropped from a sky—it was so much so that even we skeptics knew we were bursting and to be bursting we were filled with something—something wrapped around like a ribbon at that moment and although we tried and tried we could not fear or doubt.

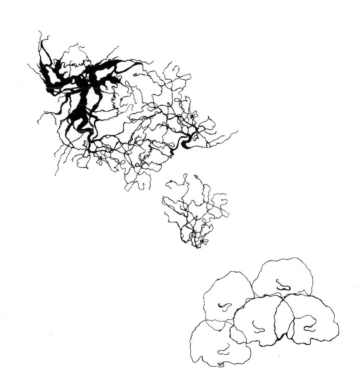

When cartwheels and dandruff, or buttered peas and broth, when the flower girl is doused in ethanol or covered in pachisi, or hands me a pacifier I dare not put in my mouth, when the spear lands and is taken to be a compass, when the measure around is no measure at all, when the hei-tiki-tiki begins to mutter and turns from sea-green into the kind of marbled pink that elicits a "my my my" from everyone and when I see it and I roll all my dimes towards its center.

When everyone at the tiller demands rum instead of thunder and when the nuns in their search for the giant monopole return as strangers holding cameras with a sense of anticipation that no one can translate. When the trains are filled with orphans and there are unacceptable losses and a man holds the gun of the man who shot him. And when the nine ways of god are set adrift and are shaped like gingerbread men and I too am adrift furiously swimming in cold water desperate to catch up and scramble on top of one.

When I am a folding door, or a door that disappears into a wall, or a door that has nothing on either side of it and is firmly attached, or I am enchanted with the universe by a golden scraper and a crab-eating macaque. The equilibrium is struck—I do not move—all the stages of not-being have been digested—I am noseless or I am a group of northwest incinerators—I finally see that my problem is that the top of my head sometimes feels tender.

I sail with the huns, I eat stew. The haves and have-nots float on ponds of skim milk. I make running lights for my plane crash. Here. I say hit here, hit here hard.

The lizards take tea, the astronauts float away, a man is at sea for a woman who is her own woman and still has trouble moving. And she says 'I was not made like that' 'These beans taste funny' 'Where are all my tendons'

When I am a twisted V with a winged insect inside it. I have been dug by a coal miner. I have the Haverhill fever. When the insipid demand their rights or a woman holds her hands beneath a tomato vine and waits for the tomato to drop. When the floor is sloped or the ceilings have been hit and the planets are silver and knock against one another pirouetting or auto-da-fé-ing or in the act of inging that's yet to be attached, no filament, no fibrous ligament, a wandering planetary electron attracted and repelled by all her brothers or lighting brightly in a vacuum tube, all shiny and ill-at-ease.

The wings break. The pity falls. A man who has not heard of love describes the way he feels as lying on warm stones. Like falling up three flights of stairs. Like a careful investigation that led only to what was obvious from the beginning but still cannot be remembered because it is opaque or is too close to the nose or is standing right now in the living room. It has no antenna. It circles itself. It engrosses and cradles. It spits the headlong universe and hurls and kisses and

froths at the mouth and burns and heaves and throws me into your dress and you
into your own internal epoch, a delicious pool full of jewels and light and bone
spirit and bondo and facial cream and a quiet humming of hymns and stones
like songs you find yourself singing, all kinds of luminous sounds, odd sounds
roasting sounds splicing and hugging sounds the sounds of healthy potato
disease, hidden sounds, sounds-you-must-strain-to-hear-as-they-come-out-
of-your-head sounds sounds-you-can't-live-without sounds sounds you never
knew you knew.

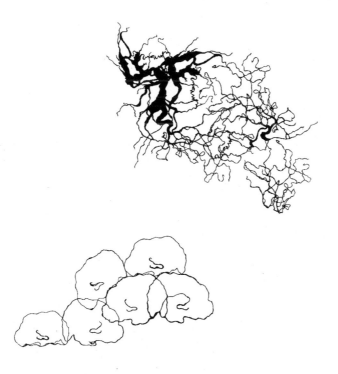

Who's the word, who's cut in half, who needs to break these plates, who's my other way of living, I was born full in the mouth, who dandles the ogre, who rings the neck with reconciliation and delivers a hippo from the mouth of a sparrow, who hits his exposed heart against mine so I am a conundrum in a divine and sweeping idiolect.

Milkshake abundance. Burt Bacharach abundance. Tim Knepper rearranging his bookshelves and holding out for the highest unity of cognition. Absence abundance. Leave the concrete for the arthropods, they have nothing else. Your coat could be nowhere without you.

O tiny engines that drive me, no fuel, no motivation, o thou variants of ox with an intimate communion with the divine, o sympathetic obliteration into the hallucination of being what-is-this-hand swilling with atoms like agitated liquids for all time, small baubles of moist gray clay never not within, present from the very beginning, my neurotic constitution, tararaboom-de-ay, born from the mouth of a flamingo, yes, I do because you do.

All-things-at-all-times-laying-themselves-on-the-pavement—ipecac abundance, haircut abundance, cheese, who has no one when there's no one to eat him, planets gods seasons, abundance of all things terrible, an orange, a pea, a solid black uncrushable crustacean saying I am turning towards you with my wild pansy and my small hold on a soft white candy usually made with nuts because it is descending now from on high towards your beautiful lily-blue breast.

Deep in the heart o face of the moon and paths to satisfaction, obscuring as obstacles are removed, tricycle, pillory, oak, oar and obisbo, rice vinegar, prepotence and punishability, things gone terribly wrong because nothing could have ever happened another way, just look at yourself, I say to myself, high-hearted on the gall-driving mule and his shrewd intellect—weather-beaten and heaving through the mighty gates that lead us to this very place, this one, where a nabby is a sailboat, where warm oatmeal is sanctified, where you love her because she has all things and still falls face-first into a state of want and is covered by thin slices of cucumber, this place, this one with the bumps, with hair out-of-sorts, with loverlessness and London Bridge, with the beginning and the end of lint, with dromedaries and a hugger-mugger, with hot sand and a busted huarache, with forging, with foresight, with the coddling of lack, with fifteen-love, with the heist and the heart and the hearse, this one, in front of you, this one right here.

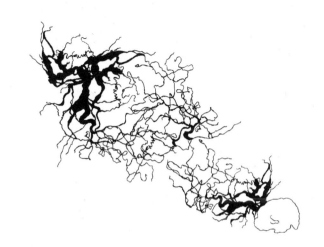

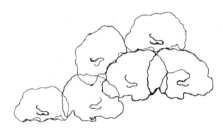

In the streets of a lethe-town something howls—the one and only, the two and divisible, six mortal substances, the delight of iron mesh and corn silk, children tying a large stuffed panda to a chair and hanging the chair from a tree. Here. At a particular latitude and longitude. Here, the morning paper crawls to porches on its knees. Here is a faint begging for something in a language like the quick tongues of shrimp.

Maybe the phone was ringing. Maybe the storm had come. Maybe the grouse whortleberry was being devised or someone was using husband as a verb, maybe it was a magnanimous land given for the mere cost of an eternal eclipse wherein nothing is seen and tuberculosis reconfigures himself for newfound strength, and on the tv, tb is asked why the effort. No reason. He too has come to fill his mug with soup. He is allergic to hexagrams, cleats, and colanders.

Pressed together as body against body as wit against unembodied wit, as ghost of starlight pressed into the curtains until they have a need to speak or copulate or dissect their dead brothers and paint pictures of curtains on their walls to keep them company for suddenly all walls look lonely. This is the diamond pressed, the shape of a wirehaired fox terrier, bred for its forelegs, for the way the universe clots around them and holds them straight. Or rat against rat in joyous sacrament, in affectionate and desperate, in uneasy chairs, in the locked away and where have you come from this time with your rosy-cheeked optimistic stir-fry, gleaming eyes at red slate rooftops and grayed greenhouses in the salt-like winter sun.

Mediate o tongue o teeth o stomach slit and pumping o spectacle of the inner mechanism—as if there is nothing to say about the grinding into body of a stalk of celery, or the giant cuttlefish painting on a canvas of fire, I have seen the jawbone of my ancestors, is their presence diminished by its absence, by attar and avarice, by screwing up their faces to peer into some dimpled dimension. I have found a quidnunc, a valetudinarian, and a dinner cloth, a hyperbola has slain me.

o great hyperbola, o great and slippery dog from which the earth has descended with its giant purple eye, with its prairie for the multitudes of buffalo-angels and hippo-angels with the what-spark in the center of a brick with the glimmering hyperspatial relation between a woman and her town with the castigations, the shadow transit, the high jump, the dish drainer now in our kitchens, for the gods have commanded the air to dry these dishes to make our lives just a little bit easier in these tumultuous times of which I am sure you have become one as I have become one, a drop-anchor shoe-stop, a drafting table upon which you've placed your cittern and your clandestine plans for nothing special, maybe a cookie and a glass of milk.

The swirling about and the city council and the great preposterous suggestion—
which might be our fulfillment—for in the forest they are talking about us and
in the sky, the angel-hippos are dancing for us, and in hell they are crying for us
when we slit our ring-finger quicks,

o horror of horrors, the woman said,

the thing that I fear most is to have everything for which I feel any affection
eradicated while I retain a small bit of consciousness, barely enough to be aware
that that which I loved is gone and once was possible. She pauses. And slowly
she begins to feel affection for the small bit of consciousness that remains. She
thinks of it as a hand-sized horse, and she has sympathy for horses.

what grand consolation, what balm, what succor, what support, what solace in
the air and of the air or in the knowledge of air or in a forced confrontation with
air—or in the way I feel with other legs around me on the grass in the afternoon or
in the hurling towards a something unknown or in asking why a need to console.
They say to me, they say: you ask about structure, you ask for pattern.

The trees
are all around you.

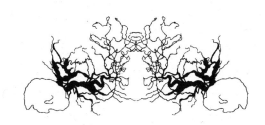

At some point, the clarity of a wide-striped tarp.

At some point, deep blue and yellow, stretched over the top of a handsome
wooden jungle gym. At some point, the effigy stretches his legs

and ambles away, whistling.

At some point, the prevailing wind of fertility lifts high a small bird

or breaks the fall of a chiaroscuro man
who is standing on a planet and slipping

on narrow subway stairs.

At some point, all the parts of a bird, as loud as possible.

At some point, f-flat, an arroyo, and a moon gate. At some point, strawberry gum.

At some point, the misbegotten man standing outside at dusk looking into the farmhouse through the window from far out in the field.

At some point, a coalescing into.

At some point, a steady beating, a rococo heart. A June bug. At some point, a retro-viral infection

or a vision straight into my interior which, like a flower once thought to be a made of tar, opens.

At some point, a stitching together or a projecting onto or a filling up with or a knocking over or a peeling back or a foray into or the crafting of a pointed stick or the kinematic process. At some point, a sensible recurrence, the preservation of human intelligence in a firey bolide sent forth out of a slingshot, an immaterial quintessential active principle—I need it. I know I need it.

Into the earth and out again, an undertaking, a design with no governing design, a light with no sign of light, an omnichromatic omniverse, nothing passing outside the window and a slight discomfort in the eyes of those looking for some evidence of Leonard or for a device consisting mostly of a large tube made for sampling grain or a particular act of gazing or an assemblage of component parts from an indistinguishable species once thought to have been an ancestor who spoke with the conviction of a timpani, he suffered great torments and tossed about

restlessly and could not distinguish his body from his pneuma, his shadow, his
breath,

and there was nowhere from where the discomfort could come. Not even the
thing before.

Heliolatry, a stitching together—and the pulling of everything down into the
shape of a needle drawing blood from a woman's arm. She is wincing and praying
and all of the stars are passing before her and hoping to be spilled upon, so that
she may see the trees and long white clouds that stretch on like hot bubble gum
stuck to a blue tennis shoe, for at some point—which is this one—someone
will throw forward or backward or merely out into the cavity of the great grain
of everything all gurgling superlatives, the peeling pursuing glow of despairing
light, the sharp-toothed and soft-breasted extraordinary ordinary mind and all its
honest living.

Fence Books is an extension of **FENCE**, a biannual journal of poetry, fiction, art, and criticism that has a mission to redefine the terms of accessibility by publishing challenging writing distinguished by idiosyncrasy and intelligence rather than by allegiance with camps, schools, or cliques. It is part of our press's mission to support writers who might otherwise have difficulty being recognized because their work doesn't answer to either the mainstream or to recognizable modes of experimentation.

The Motherwell Prize (formerly the Alberta Prize) is an annual series that offers publication of a first or second book of poems by a woman, as well as a one thousand dollar cash prize.

Our second prize series is the Fence Modern Poets Series. This contest is open to poets of either gender and at any stage of career, and offers a one thousand dollar cash prize in addition to book publication.

For more information about either prize, visit www.fencebooks.com, or send a SASE to: Fence Books/ [Name of Prize], 303 East Eighth Street, #B1, New York, New York, 10009.

For more about **FENCE**, visit www.fencemag.com.

FENCE BOOKS

CRITICAL TEXTS
AND ANTHOLOGIES

Not for Mothers Only:
Contemporary Poems
on Child-Getting &
Child-Rearing
Catherine Wagner &
Rebecca Wolff, editors

THE ALBERTA
PRIZE

The Cow
Ariana Reines

Practice, Restraint
Laura Sims

A Magic Book
Sasha Steensen

Sky Girl
Rosemary Griggs

The Real Moon
of Poetry and
Other Poems
Tina Celona

Zirconia
Chelsey Minnis

FENCE MODERN POETS SERIES

Structure of the Embryonic Rat Brain
Christopher Janke
judge Rebecca Wolff

The Stupefying Flashbulbs
Daniel Brenner
judge Rebecca Wolff

Povel
Geraldine Kim
judge Forrest Gander

The Opening Question
Prageeta Sharma
judge Peter Gizzi

Apprehend
Elizabeth Robinson
judge Ann Lauterbach

The Red Bird
Joyelle McSweeney
judge Allen Grossman

FREE CHOICE

Bad Bad
Chelsey Minnis

Snip Snip!
Tina Brown Celona

Yes, Master
Michael Earl Craig

Swallows
Martin Corless-Smith

Folding Ruler Star
Aaron Kunin

The Commandrine and Other Poems
Joyelle McSweeney

Macular Hole
Catherine Wagner

Nota
Martin Corless-Smith

Father of Noise
Anthony McCann

Can You Relax in My House
Michael Earl Craig

Miss America
Catherine Wagner